Leaning on a Blue Door

poems by

Alice Lee Timmins

Finishing Line Press
Georgetown, Kentucky

Leaning on a Blue Door

*For my beloved ancestors
whose stories are mine.*

"Ancestors"

Copyright © 2025 by Alice Lee Timmins
ISBN 979-8-88838-916-4 First Edition
All rights reserved under International and Pan-American Copyright Conventions. No part of this book may be reproduced in any manner whatsoever without written permission from the publisher, except in the case of brief quotations embodied in critical articles and reviews.

ACKNOWLEDGMENTS

The Poet is Grateful to the following publications in which several of the poems in this collection previously appeared:

"Breathing Underwater": in *Piscataqua Poems 2*; also in another format in *The Fourth River*
"Cradle": in *The Aurorean*
"Floral Fields": *Lunation*
"A New Map": by Exsolutas Press *Thriving*.
"Opening Testimony": in *Cutthroat 29 Journal*
"Signals Lost": in *Good Fat Poetry* Zine
"Puddle Dock Cottages": in *Piscataqua Poems 2*

    I thank first editor, Brian Evans-Jones (Former Poet Laureate of Hampshire, UK, now residing in New Hampshire, US.) His keen discernment, amazing sense of order, rhythm and context has shepherded this poet's writing thus far.
    I am grateful to my mentor, Kimberly Cloutier Green (Former Poet Laureate of Portsmouth, NH). Her encouragement in writing workshops and on our brisk walks has reinvigorated my writing practice.
    New England poets of *The Kittery Art Association*'s "Tuesday Poetry Circle" (Kittery, ME) and poets of the *Historic New England*'s "The Sarah Orne Jewett Monday Writers' Circle" (South Berwick, ME) gave a broad forum for ongoing critique of my poems.
    My toughest critics (and most humorous supporters) Aimée C. Timmins, and Margaret A. Cook, massaged each poem through final revisions. I am indebted to them.
    I thank Aimée C. Timmins and Dawn Reynolds Graves whose artworks grace this book.

Publisher: Leah Huete de Maines
Editor: Christen Kincaid
Cover Art: "Nuthatch" by Aimee Catherine Timmins
Author Photo: Margaret A. Cook
Cover Design: Elizabeth Maines McCleavy

Order online: www.finishinglinepress.com
also available on amazon.com

Author inquiries and mail orders:
Finishing Line Press
PO Box 1626
Georgetown, Kentucky 40324
USA

Contents

Section One ~Beneath the Surface

The Bell of Awareness 2
Fusion 3
Unmoored Dreams 4
Breathing Underwater 5
Human Clay 6
Tucked In 7
Mapled in Reds 8
Finch Aria 9
Cradle 11
Spouting Rock 12
Photographic Memory 14
The Ice Man 15
Just a Pie Plate 16
Floral Fields 17
Ancestral Dream 18
Inklings of Rosa 19
Unlatched 20
A New Map 21

Section Two ~ Wide-Angle Lens

Opening Testimony 23
In the Rushes 25
Dispatches 26
Escort 28
Voyager 29
Signals Lost 30
Kepler 31
Beldon, England 1940 32
Puddle Dock Cottages 33
All this Stirring 34

Book Notes 35

Section One ~ Beneath the Surface

"Surfaces"

The Bell of Awareness
(cento)

Through a pitch-dark limitless grove
witness the foaming turbulence
of a river.
We gather the pine cones

bright green and immature
let them dry in an airy place,
I join my palms and let a flower bloom
wonderfully in my heart.
          Deeper into matter.

For as long as the sun shall have risen
and the rivers go down to the sea
the earth's magnetic field
has reversed polarity.
We are stardust brought to life,
empowered to figure itself out.
          Or is it something more subtle?

The bird celebrating life
among older hawthorn trees,
gnarled twigs covered with lichen
in different hues,
The truth moving behind the surface of things…
The bell of awareness
begins to sound.

(Excerpts: The Alcatraz Proclamation to the Great White Father and his People, 1969; M. Mitchell Waldrop, Kenneth C. Davis, Edle Catharina Norman, Thich Nhat Hanh, Eileen Caddy of Findhorn, Neil DeGrasse Tyson, Meinrad Craighead.)

Fusion

A tectonic shift,
an alchemic stir,
a singular glance,
this suddenly *her*.

This prescient knowing,
this fusion of touch,
such clarity of Who
creating an *Us*.

This ancient desire,
this confessional *Yes*,
the physics of night,
and this bone deep rest.

Unmoored Dreams

Like a summer child
you fling off formal skin
Race into the wildness of
surfacing fins,
feathered wings,
hovering over and under, you swim.
I do remember your unremembered dreams.

Tamer nights are set in lecture halls,
at podiums
behind convent walls.
Fingertips rise
pointing to a cloud.
You want to go abroad,
say *Amsterdam* aloud.
You list your fervent needs,
demand the keys.

Agitated sleep of a
fogged-in sailor,
you squint and wait.
Troubles ghosting in,
unrequited sorrows,
unforgiven slights,
a thousand untold sins.
Teeth clenched,
you claw, rip, kick,
encased in rage—you scream.

Morning breaks the tremulation,
images dissolve
Your smile—intimate,
calm oblivion.
But unmoored,
and in pieces, I
hand press the bed clothes,
calm my racing pulse.
My echoing ears do remember
      your unremembered dreams.

Breathing Underwater

Out on Star Island's windward rocky ledge,
I don't remember crossing here,
there may have been a boat.
I float along a sandy trail,
fog polishing the Atlantic dawn,
then the pull and collapse of an old chant:
a bell buoy moaning on a wide wave swell.
Gulls tip and etch the air,
leathery black cormorants dip and disappear.

At a beach outcrop between cliffs
I take the risk, wade out
feet cooling in a receding wave,
liquid sand rushing beneath my heels,
I'm sliding backward—somewhere deeper.
    The *sploosh* of an oar
    a white dory glides in from the mist.
    The chance meeting of an Adonis figure.
    An unknown twin? A brother, or a lover,
    or both?
        We tread calmly,
        become rosy-tangerine with the sunset,
         dip in unison below the surface,
        speak secrets breathing underwater.
            Coral rays play through him as
            he dissolves in submerged indigo.

Memory? Fantasy?
—I don't know.
There is a song coming from the dock.
Lucid and back on land I
squint back at the *Thomas Leighton* tour boat
the re-embarking of tired, sunburnt mainland day visitors.
I turn slowly away,
think my way out of my
sweaty hiking clothes,
dive deep
        and grow fins.

Human Clay

We could talk of
fury aiming Paris' arrow,
of Achilles' heel,
of Orion's sword.
But these are tensions far away,
others' ancient chaos.

I say
—put down your keys, your bag
       Tell me what tide pulls you away,
Give me back your amber eyes, your human clay.

You speak of the waning moon's light diminishing
with such clarifying insight.
I pause as our pulses untwine,
two torn mortals
totally spent,
leaning
on a blue door.

Tucked In

These humus Maine woods
our home cloaked in Spring birdsong.
Dry morning air arrives like news
weathering us into the summer.
Moist August mornings
steep us like tea.
That boardwalk of hand-hewn cedar
beckons us to the river,
but it needs repair.
Hard work polishes us through late Autumn.
Crisp winter crinkles its dappling shards.
We light the wood stove, our tap root,
and welcome in that rare bit of company:
trail advice, wine, stories, mostly laughter,
the song where we belong.
Then, like a silent chime everywhere in New England,
good guests go.
One of us clicks closed the screen door,
flips off the front lights.
Tucked into our lichen-tinted cottage,
this is where we lay our heads,
where we mark the page,
where we choose to age.

Mapled in Reds

It does my heart good, Jacquie,
autumn is gleaming ablaze
on this crisp drive home toward Maine.
I was broken in New Jersey,
touching your smooth brow,
caressing the soft skin between your slender fingers,
whispering, lingering,
burying you in rosaries and ritual.

Now my car crests the Piscataqua Bridge,
beech leaves paint the highway north,
I take the backroad home through Eliot.
A low angular sundown stains maple leaves to brilliant tangerine,
birch leaves rain down like vireos,
I can hear our last phone call—
your certainty—*I'll see you in the Fall.*

Turning at the line of mailboxes onto
York Woods Road,
lit through shards of yellow and russet
I crisscross a familiar purple forest,
float the last supple mile home
confettied in winterberries,
  your eyes—
papered in sumac,
  your slender fingers—
everywhere mapled in falling reds
  your voice.
How prescient you were
  I see you—in—the Fall.

Finch Aria

I take the dirt road left
along a margin of dusty scrub oaks
and pleated beech leaves,
a listening pace—soft even steps
drumming the evening road.
Out on a quivering branch,
A yellow tuxedo in full finch view,
his open furtive throat wiggling grace notes,
scattering flecks of golden sound.
His simple stanza flicks the sky,
        Nine notes rising
        quickening
        a descant popping aloft.

My toe barely scuffs the road.
This careless puff
sprays dozens of frenetic finches
out of these beeches,
a disarray of
        harps, strings, bows
        flinging up, fanning out
        stirring the air with a palpable
        trilling, trilling, trilling.

They re-assemble in mid-flight
low over South Berwick powerlines,
their allegro swerves under,
then sky rolls over the wires.
Finally the flock kites across the meadow.
They choose a hefty white pine,
well away from boots and roads,
finches pour as one into the branches
camouflaged in pine needles.
A long rest note,
conspiratorial silence.

I steady my feet, tilt and cup my ear
'til faintly, softened by distance,
There—a singular voice, that hypnotic scale,
nine notes piping, ascending,
one singular finch aria pierces the meadow.

Eventually, but not yet,
the soft rhythm of my leather boots
will accompany me home.

Cradle

Coaxed by pulsing muscles,
hidden muffled voices.
Born mammal
awash in milk and blood
flood of floods.
Pressed into the world desperately naked
lowing for her breast,
cradled there
I rest.

Six decades later.
A solitary afternoon.
An antique shop's dusty corners,
its vintage hoardings.
My savory surprise:
a disconnected rotary phone.
I finger the coil,
I cradle its hefty black handle to my ear.
That tone.
Those long unused, still remembered
ten numerals.
I dial
Person—to—Person
I am calling home.

Spouting Rock

I pull the car along the tight shoulder of Parson's Way
and park.
It's been fifty years:
we five kids scrambling on a rocky rim,
Dad lighting and relighting a cigar,
his big hands help us bait and cast,
we wiggle and wait—and mind the tide.
Mom's navy blue headscarf corrals brunette hair.
On the single bench through Jackie O sunglasses,
she reads.
She's set off from us a bit
windblown and lovely.

~

Now I roll down the window, hear the surf,
the tide too full to spout,
I'm thinking back two decades:
Dad's time folding in on him,
His voice   —*Promise me you'll care for her,*
                  will you do this for me?

I gather items from the front seat,
thinking now to just this passing month:
Mom asking—*Out to sea like Dad's?*—*Oh, but Ireland is so far…*
I offered—*Mom, would you like me to return you to New England?*
Her relief—*Yes, that's it, back to Spouting Rock,*
                  will you do this for me?

~

I'm standing near her bench awash in…
those conversations … promises kept…
Ireland seems not so far, nearly in view …
I wait 'til Spouting Rock begins to pound away
high tide roaring out.
Her ashes sift the air, skein into the Atlantic
on a massive swell.
Two tossed yellow dahlias sail off with the ebb
far beyond rocks and … me.
I reach for their names, their stories, a sense of …

Lingering, a bit lost,
I caress my pocketed car keys
It's time to leave
this sacred shore.

Photographic Memory

I once sat on the edge of Saturn counting braided rings,
millions of failed moons,
that was before my birthtime.

Once as a child, an *Eagle* landed on our moon.
I watched it *live* in black and white, Pawnee Street,
three generations staring at a grainy screen
seeing the impossible in a new Bethlehem.

Once I hailed a tiny skiff off Parson's Beach,
tide was a fast receding river,
but being only nine I was simply an amusement,
easy to wave off.

Once I gleaned Hermit Island sand dollars,
Aunt Mary placed these in a very serious shoebox,
gems to be hidden under my bed.
By spring I tenderly spread these around Maryland azaleas.

My memories a clear lens
zooming out and back.
With 'rapt focus,
often in slow motion,
I learn from my future
and make my plans
with long dead kin.

The Ice Man

Pepére's solid gaze
unraveled many on Lincoln Street.
He rarely spoke in full voice
but sang softly while delivering ice and fresh muffins
out the back of a steam-converted hay truck.

Evenings, his black Packard trundled
down Marlborough's main street and into back alleys.
There was the Lake William Tavern,
a line of dark shiny cars in front by 8pm,
patron's drinking windowless blue air,
a muffled piano trying to shine the moon of '32.
Pepére would float through the front room,
knock and wait at the back.
A hole—a shard of light—a telling nod.
Where errand boys with leather pouches
learned not to ask questions,
phone calls and runners in and out,
decks of cards and inky record books,
horse and greyhound ratings,
nicknames and everyone's cousin: *Bookie*.

Memére rarely mentioned the back alleys,
those smoky rooms.
His lake ice and her baked goods were always delivered on time.
Fridays Pepére brought home a wallet stuffed with cash,
his pockets filled with penny candy for the three children.

There was that night at home off Silver Street
the phone rang,
An unknown throaty voice with a message from Pepére.
She hadn't learned to drive,
but Memére whisked the toddlers out to the garage,
put the car in neutral and rolled them right down French Hill
past the patrol car.
Pepére came home late that night
with his arresting confidence that held
her breath, her waist—
his eyes with answers to all her questions.

Just a Pie Plate

Tires on crushed gravel getting close.
Few ever meander these woods,
cross the earthen bridge,
lose themselves far enough to come upon our cottage.
I check the corner window.
A little cobalt blue car.
Can it be—her?
Harmless, and beautiful—and here?
She is turning the vehicle in our drive.
Perhaps she's unsure,
perhaps it is curiosity?
I hurry out, no—*fling myself* toward the fact of her,
send out her name through the rain.

Then red brake lights.
She lowers the window with a smile,
hands me a thank you note with
a returned pie plate.
I say—We're all here, come in.
There is a long hesitant moment,
then the swipe of delayed wipers.
Her voice is soft
No … it was the pie plate,
 … it took so long to find you,
 … I cannot be long.
I say—
        Come back soon for dinner, we never lock the door.
But this is my Crush, not hers.
She's happy in her world,
I am in mine.
We two
cannot
belong.

Floral Fields

There's a feel to the rain on a warm spring day
that's so brand new,
it rolls in with a storm, now it's on its way,
I'm surrounded by you.

There's a song in the air, a softening hue,
a brush—a kiss—a sigh,
your tenor lilt, your sweet sad face,
those Irish blue eyes.

Gentlemen songsters off on a spree!
That was what you sang to me,
Lord have mercy on such as we—by and by.

Where, oh where, is my Icabod Crane,
how will his horse get him out of this rain?
He was kind, confused, and he'd lost his way
he reminds me of you.

There's a place in the heart on that longest night,
The saying of goodbye.
I close my eyes 'til burns a light,
You are emeralding the sky.

Are the *Whiffenpoof* assembled,
are their glasses raised on high,
does the trace of a cigar kiss the air?
Has that little black sheep finally found his way
in the floral fields there?

There's a tug on the wind from far away,
an old familiar tune,
It's a prayer washed by a warm spring rain,
It's the song of you.

Ancestral Dream

Somewhere in June was a lullaby,
suddenly you are here,
a certain look now in your parents' eyes,
Heaven and Earth in a prayer.
All the King's Horses, the dish and the spoon
can't still my heart as it beats for you.

Rivers of glass in wintertime,
strap on ice skates and fly.
The stars twirl above like big cow eyes,
if you ask—they may even tell why.
"Hey diddle-diddle" the Milky Way giggles
as Little Boy Blue skates to the moon.

Where are you headed, what do you wish?
The full moon lights the trees.
Cast your net wherever you wish,
fish the ancestral stream.
Panpipes chime an impossible tune,
and gently rock you to sleep.

Somewhere in June was a lullaby,
suddenly you are here.
The leaf on our Tree,
the future alive,
you—an ancestral dream.

Inklings of Rosa

She faced a warm August sun,
she wore a bold Spanish rose,
she laughed the way she danced,
and the World beneath her spun.

It feels as though the Earth has slowed its gentle roll a bit,
Morning air is tangled in the branches, things don't fit.
The certainty of a song, and the guitar strings all have quit,
it feels as though the planet has slowed its gentle roll a bit.

The entirety beneath her feet finally gave way.
As if the music has slowed,
as though colors aren't as bold,
our conversation now grows old.
We've lost a Love, it's real, it's here,
Deep silence everywhere.

So given time and a few strong storms,
given rest, when the resting comes,
we'll water our lives with what we've learned,
'til again our petals face the sun,

recall her laughter, her outline, her voice,
the warmth of her name, her look, her way.
The air will waft with a Spanish refrain,
and the days will revolve as they once did when

she faced a warm August sun
and wore a bold Spanish rose,
She laughed the way she danced,
and the Earth beneath her spun.

Unlatched

It's an hour before dusk.
She runs in an athletic rhythm,
heart rate steady, a holding pattern.
It's a worn path along Winslow's farm,
timed for her to return precisely before sundown.
She strides familiar creek stones,
over the iron gate,
one lap around the frog pond,
the final warmup for Half Mile Hill.
She sweats past milkweed pods, goldenrod and chicory,
to the barn, then the main house.
She checks her pulse, her watch—then turns for home.

But the June air has unlatched something,
She tilts her head …
Clink, scrape, tink—
and stops.
A cupola window topping the barn
has loosened,
hinged glass panes have swung open
releasing a yellow cloud glinting early evening's light.
Sulfur butterflies madly pour free—beating at the cool air,
pale buttery wings skein out
over the pond,
circling rabbit foot clover,
their airy diaspora wilding the sky.

She stands still in the meadow.
Tall grass redolent of honeysuckle,
silhouetted trees chiming with vireos, cardinals, finch.
Her body suddenly saturated,
with fresh senses she catches at last
the minute-hand
of the departing sun.

A New Map

Early June
Maine woods
Margaret is out deadheading daffodils,
weeding foxgloves, clearing lily-of-the-valley,
cutting iris fans.
Vintage coral poppies push bold heads up;
yet these perennials are suddenly mysterious to her
    We must have planted them last October, a lovely surprise.
    And which way to the river?
Our garden path trips her
where twelve summers ago we lifted, placed flat stones.

An unlatched window?
A door ajar?
The vault of her memories somehow has unbolted?
Absorbed with making sense of ongoing lapses
we learn its name—Alzheimers.
Will it carve away our history,
level our Colorado,
    wring the rain from Paris,
        fell these Maine woods?

Late September
the map is new,
Our garden path evaporates, then
re-morphs each morning.
Whose and *Who* are confused
sometimes I am *Alice*,
sometimes I am *Doris*,
or a kind person steadying her.
Always she is Margaret to me.
Determined, I slow my own ticking clock
in tandem with her precious mind,
the humble *now*,
in present imperfect tense.

Section Two ~ *Wide-Angle Lens*

"Micro—Macro—Wide Angle"

Opening Testimony
(cento in two voices)

I am here
    Oh beautiful
Not because I want to be,
    America
I am terrified
    America.
I believe it is my duty to tell you
    for pilgrims' feet
what happened to me, the impact on my life.
    Mountain majesties.
I met the boy
    for heroes proved
who sexually assaulted me
    for patriots' dream.
The details have been seared
    God shed his grace
into my memory
    amber waves
and have haunted me episodically as an adult
    that see beyond the years.
I was pushed from behind,
    in self control
there was loud music playing,
    undimmed by human tears
I was pushed on the bed,
    America, America
he got on top of me
    for freedom's ring
I tried to yell
    for halcyon skies
he put his hand over my mouth.
    in liberating strife
it was hard for me to breathe,
    as earth and air
I thought he was accidentally going to kill me.
    for man's avail
Both were drunkenly laughing
    with brotherhood
they seemed to be having

>   *through wilds of thought*
> a very good time.
> They went pin-balling off the walls
>   *who more than self their country love*
> loudly down the stairs
>   *and mercy more than life.*
> Indelible was the laughter.
>   *Oh Beautiful, oh America!*
> I am terrified.

(Excerpts from the Christine Blasey Ford testimony Oct. 2, 2018 to the Senate Judiciary Committee's 2nd Hearing for a New Supreme Court Justice; lyrics from Katharine Lee Bates' "America the Beautiful.")

In the Rushes
—*Rakhine State, Myanmar*

Wind rustles the osiers here by the Bay of Bengal.
A young woman follows a worn path,
her hajib crimson-stained,
her smoking village a burnt memory.
Hidden by tall rushes
she checks the midday sun,
rearranges her newborn bundle,
tiny lips pulling breast milk.
Vigilantly, she listens,
patiently, she waits,
hums, plays with his fingers,
he coos,
she prays
… *O Prophets in the wild* …

By evening the slap of an oar.
A single monk's figure
appears
shoring his wooden boat.
… *O Siddhartha, be the boatman.*
A quiet look into one another's eyes,
she opens her palm of coins.
He gently waves it away,
guides them onto a crude wooden seat,
nearly silent he rows two tired passengers
away.

Wind rustles the osiers by the Bay of Bengal.

Dispatches

Stars drop from the flag.
Pendulum frozen, polarized
This is not a drill,
    Break Glass.

Final dispatch
American journalist slain in a sanctuary.
His fiancée's vigil, raw grief
an amulet for the news cycle
    This Just In

Ghostly-white angry *jungen*
snaking about campus,
gripping lit torches,
left their white hoods behind,
    You will not replace us.

Hats and ties and gloves and purses
Ballot lines to Black Churches
winding the block for hours.
Closed until further notice.
    Deliver us

School intercom
We have an active shooter!
Look for the helpers
Shelter in place
    Run, Hide, Fight

Elections matter
Black lives matter
Say Their Names
…Trayvon … Breonna …George
    <*insert name here*>

Ticking packages,
Handwritten addresses—ALL CAPS,
fused and synchronized in the morning mail,
    See Something, Say Something.

Miles of southern border razor wire
caged children in the desert,
No one out or in.
    Pray for us sinners

The last page of American democracy
archived in numberless dispatches,
American story
of the fall.

Escort

They sent me.
They sent a small solemn bird
to blend with plague pandemonium,
so many leavings, solitary snatchings,
un-chorused departures,
lonesome goodbyes.

At the mad fact of your own sudden dying,
your invisible escort
I hover inches over your final breath,
circle silently near your cooling skin,
my current of air your last touch
in crossing over.

Your hurried burial
I am that flicker of song
marking your remains, the grave
for those who will come
in their own black cloth
when the *All Clear* is sounded.

Now I tie loose silver ribbons about your essence,
lift each strand with my beak,
my indigo eyes navigate midnight clouds,
portage you to your next promised sky.
I cannot linger here,
they are sending for me
again.

Voyager
      (haibun)

The little spacecraft had a camera, an earpiece, and a transmitter. To explore the planets, NASA propelled *Voyager* beyond Earth's orbit. The year was 1979. For two decades she neared each middle planet capturing unprecedented sounds and photos. Her transmissions lit up receivers and screens back on Earth. The sounds crackly, the images grainy black and white; but it was the mid-twentieth century and everything was still so amazing. More decades passed. Higher resolution devices on newer crafts were launched making *Voyager* obsolete. Or was she? Etched in golden grooves on her metallic skin were inscribed messages: a calling card of art, music, science, of peace, and a map locating Earth in its galaxy. Rather than shut her off, fine minds hatched a bold plan. She could take a one-way flight beyond the solar system. But how to leave? *Voyager* was instructed to use Jupiter's gravity as a slingshot. At unimaginable velocity, she careened around the burly planet. Physics flung her on an outward trajectory leaving the distant planets and sun's gravity behind. Now she sails on pure inertia; and she is still recording. Screens at Mission Control await her faint signals. Day after day, year after year, Earthlings listen, watch, in hope that the little spacecraft may become someone else's revelation. That *Voyager* might one day transmit its ongoing story back home.

An unlatched gate
little lamb blinks and blinks
leaps to the open field.

Tending shepherd squints
listens for a **baa, a bleat**
keeps the gate open this night.

Signals Lost

Odd quiet in the dimming light,
wood thrush pipes gone missing,
chipmunks have burrowed or crept away,
empty woods,
nothing stays
but silence
encircling forest, town,
this green blue sphere.

Now the lines to Europe are being cut
signals lost,
compasses spin strangely.
Veterans shake their heads
warning of an October past,
last chance to turn back.
They lie awake,
they die away.
In a mad calculus
adversaries, unencumbered by doubt,
tilt history into a brawl.
Covered Live in High Def',
pressurized nuclear suns encased in submarines,
troll these shores
and drone over on metallic wing.
This growing risk
human error, technical accident,
or malignant nod.
With a single *ping*
cables would melt,
eardrums fracture,
screens go dark.
All who breathe, sprout,
grow thumbs, hooves, wings
would burn into
a gray, thrushless
odd quiet in the dimming light.

Kepler
      (cento)

Earth has named a telescope hurtling through space
for Johannes.
Kepler, designed and tuned
to discover Earth-like planets
around Sun-like stars.

The universe is under no obligation to make sense.
The wheel turning in
a near-infinity of possible patterns
carrying us along.

In the presence of the undisturbed,
instead of sheep
[Kepler] was counting planets,
the profound mystery,
the deliciously exotic.

Moving on pure intellectual adrenaline, on insight,
on his capacity to hover over the heads of contemporaries,
he grasped a handful of pieces
saw connections,
nodded with confidence to our sun
and showed us how to steer.

(Excerpts from Robert Frost, David Gergen, Thich Nhat Hanh, Neil deGrasse Tyson, and M. Mitchell Waldrop.) Dedicated to scientist astronomer Johannes Kepler.

Beldon, England 1940

I long for the scent of the Miniver Rose, to belong to its southern English village on the river. To shake the course hands of the bell ringer, greet the station master who calls each passenger *Love*, names his rose for Kay Miniver, the loveliest. It is late May, planes overhead. An unrelenting pelting from the sky, tremors pound the cottages. The cratering of acres. I hope to be as calm and strong as the Miniver couple, tucked in an earthen shelter, soothing their child, knitting, quipping. I long to slip outside, catch a bombardier's package and hurl it back. I would hope to give an hour's rest to Clem, one of countless civilian fathers who rev their small boat engines, set out into a night that folds into a sleepless week. Complete news blackout. I would wait by the radio, watch Kay at the garden dock on that sun-soaked morning; she listens for the sputter of a battered boat engine. Squinting down river, her jaw relaxes at last. I hear them approach, she shouldering Clem into the house and up to sleep. This village of fathers who crossed the ravaged Channel again and again and again ferrying to safety their uniformed sons. When he awakens, Clem Miniver will whisper the name of a French town, Dunkirk.

Puddle Dock Cottages
(ekphrasis)

Airy streetscapes
stretched canvas,
tilted simplicity,
captured grace.

Shingled cottages
lavender tint,
shortened shadows
implying noon.

Spare palette
Naples yellow,
one teal line
defining shore.

Pale chimneys,
nowhere particular,
somehow spectacular,
everywhere a masterpiece.

All This Stirring

All these Earthly stirrings
lit candles in temples,
coins clatter measuring prayers,
pagan dances,
critics in the reserved seats toss spoiled fruit
at their own unrequited desires,
clergies weep.

Sparks stirring from campfires
measure the distance between villages.
Signal fires seeking another universe
where languages chime,
where, curling along rocky shores,
whales lift their massive voices—songhouses,
   chamber music for the lost.

All this stirring
opening scenes and credits all at once,
dreams of beautiful endings:
Michelangelo's obsession,
Borodin's Steppes,
Mahler's Adagios,
The Requiems,
and the autopsies reveal
tears on their cheeks,
something
they knew.

Illustrations credited:

Cover Illustration "*Nuthatch*", an acrylic painting printed with permission by artist Aimee C. Timmins of South Berwick, ME.

"*The Bell of Awareness*" is an art photograph by the poet digitally re-imagined.

"*Ancestors*" is an art photograph by the poet also digitally re-imagined. It appears on the dedication page.

"*Surfaces*" Section One divider page. Art photo by the artist.

"*But it Needs Repair*" is an art photograph by the poet.

"*Floral Fields*" [Ibid.]

"*Little Boy Blue*" is a photo of the poet's grandnephew to accompany the poem "Ancestral Dream." Printed with permission of the photographer, Dawn Reynolds Graves of New Windsor, MD.

"*Micro—Macro—Wide Angle*"—Section Two divider page is an art photograph by the poet. It appears after, and to accompany, Section Two.

"*The Crossing*" is an original art photo digitally re-imagined by the poet.

Alice put her early poetry in a desk file—on hold for decades. She received honors of Magna Cum Laude and Phi Beta Kappa while earning double majors in History and Anthropology from the University of Delaware; her Secondary Teaching Certification was received from Towson University and her Masters in Secondary Counseling was received from The Johns Hopkins University in Maryland. Her textured career has been service-oriented. In Washington, DC with a women's advocacy non-profit; then teaching secondary social studies in Takoma Park, Maryland; then to Denver, Colorado with her Masters in Counseling where she taught and counseled. Finally she found lifelong learners in her final position as a Coordinator of Volunteers at the Denver Art Museum. Now retired, Alice writes poetry from a sunny desk with her cat Molly Blue often draped across the keyboard, at a cottage on the Great Works River in South Berwick, Maine. Daily she walks with her partner Margaret and their beloved dog Quincy. In her early sixties, she stays young creating textile art pieces, installing artwork at the Kittery Art Association, playing pickleball, and spending long afternoons cutting firewood from their home's forest floor.

www.ingramcontent.com/pod-product-compliance
Lightning Source LLC
Chambersburg PA
CBHW042335150426
43194CB00005B/171